Jeremy Plays the Blues

May 28, 2021

Jeremy Plays the Blues

by Amy Oden Simpson

May you celebrate your own unique gifts, bringing joy and connection to others.

Illustrated by

Jeannice Jones Sanders

With love,
Amy Oden Simpson

Jeremy Plays the Blues
by Amy Oden Simpson

Illustrated by Jeannice Jones Sanders

Text & illustration copyright © 2021 Amy Oden Simpson

Published in 2021 by:
Climbing Angel Publishing
PO Box 32381, Knoxville, Tennessee 37930
www.ClimbingAngel.com

First Edition June 2021
Printed in the United States of America

Cover Layout by Tara Hayes
Interior Design by Climbing Angel Publishing
Special Illustration Editing by Shawn Williams

ISBN: 978-1-63732-619-0

To Corley & Sidney,
my inspiration.

My name is Jeremy.

My mother says that I am

a special boy.

I love to paint.

My mother says that I paint very well.

Every morning I paint with
my teacher, Miss Lauren.

When I paint,
I feel like I AM
using words.

One day, while I was painting,
Miss Lauren began to play her guitar.

She played what she
called **"the blues."**

She played songs by people named...

Muddy Waters

Ma Rainey

&

Memphis Minnie!

When I heard the music,
I grew very excited.

My body started to move
and I danced.

Then Miss Lauren began to sing,
and I began to hum.

Humming was easy for me.

My humming blended with the
sound of the guitar.

My paintings sang along too.

I painted the sounds I was hearing.

I painted faster and faster.

I looked
at my paintings
and felt joy.

Others felt joy too!

The next day
when I went to school,

Miss Lauren gave
me a present...

My very own guitar!

I thought to myself,

"I will paint it!"

And I did...

I painted my guitar **blue**!

I have found my way to
play the blues.

My mother was right.

I am a special boy!

The End

ABOUT CLIMBING ANGEL PUBLISHING

Climbing Angel Publishing exists for the purpose of sharing stories of hope and encouragement, aiding in the gathering together of community, and supporting the process of betterment. The following books are available at ClimbingAngel.com and major bookstores.

ADULT BOOKS: *(Romans 8:28-30)*

In His Image, Sam Polson (English, Romanian, & Mandarin)
By Faith, Sam Polson (English & Romanian)
My Birthday Gift to Jesus, Lisa Soland
Without Ceasing, Dr. Dennis Davidson
SonLight: Daily Light from the Pages of God's Word, Sam Polson
Corona Victus: Conquering the Virus of Fear, Sam Polson
Art Bushing: His Diary, Letters, & Photographs of WWII, Art Bushing
Art & Dotty: His Diary, Their Letters & Photographs of WWII, Art Bushing
Trimisul, Stan Johnson (Romanian)
Life Changing Prayer, Sam Polson

CHILDREN'S BOOKS: *(Philippians 4:8)*

The Christmas Tree Angel, Lisa Soland
The Unmade Moose, Lisa Soland
Thump, Lisa Soland
Somebunny To Love, Lisa Soland (English & Mandarin)
The Truth about God's Rainbow, Lisa Soland
God's Promises, Lisa Soland
The Boy & The Bagel Necklace, Lisa Soland
God's Hands and Feet, Lisa Soland
I Like To Be Quiet, Joni Caldwell
Wheels Off!, Karlie Saumier
Ella's Trip of a Lifetime, Melanie Ewbank
Because You Are Mine, Gayle Childress Greene
Jeremy Plays the Blues, Amy Oden Simpson

ELLA'S TRIP OF A LIFETIME
by Melanie Ewbank

ELLA IS A KID WHO NEEDS TO STAY ACTIVE. SHE GETS BORED EASILY. Her mom says, "Ella, you have a family of squirrels in your brain that seems to be impossible to manage." During a family vacation, Ella's impatience gets the best of her, and she tries to swim in the hotel pool by herself. Ella nearly drowns, then takes the trip of a lifetime to visit heaven. While there, she learns a lesson she will never forget!

WHEELS OFF!
by Karlie Saumier

Wheels Off! is Hazel and Henry's first of many adventures together. Henry is Hazel's little brother, who sometimes wishes he wasn't so little. While playing at the local playground, a group of bullies pick on Henry, but his sister is there to help him discover that "Heaven on Earth" is not that far away.

"A terrific Christ-inspired story of forgiveness, family, and friendship."
– Lisa Soland, author

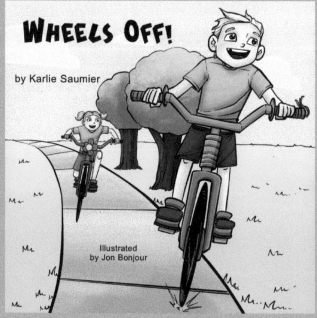

I LIKE TO BE QUIET
by Joni Caldwell

This book is written to honor *the quiet child*, the child that likes to observe, the child that enjoys a little alone time to think. Like me, I know you are amazed as you watch your quiet child. I hope this book will serve as the backdrop for you to snuggle into each other for a while. Let's make sure they know how interesting they are and how very proud we are of them, *just the way they are.*

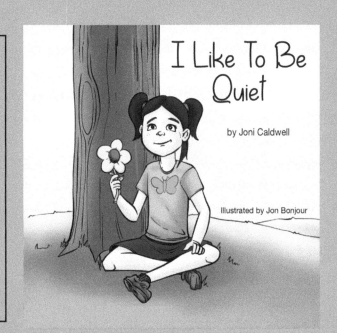

THE BOY & THE BAGEL NECKLACE
by Lisa Soland

In *The Boy and the Bagel Necklace*, Andrew, a resident of a Romanian orphanage, tells us the story of when Jesus visited him in a dream. Jesus tells Andrew not to worry, that everything is going to be all right. Soon after, the leadership in Romania changes and little Andrew is adopted and brought to America where he learns that Jesus Christ is more than just a nice man who visits desperate children in their dreams. When little Andrew learns just how much God loves him, his life is radically changed.

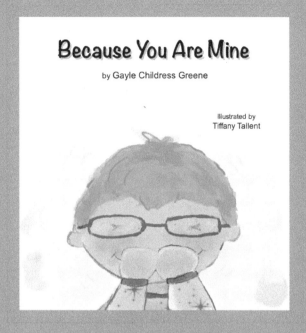

Because You Are Mine

by Gayle Childress Greene

Illustrated by
Tiffany Tallent

BECAUSE YOU ARE MINE
by Gayle Childress Greene

SHARE THE WARMTH OF BELONGING THAT CONNECTS US WITH THOSE WE LOVE IN THIS BEAUTIFULLY TOLD STORY AND ILLUSTRATED BOOK. AT NAPTIME, BEDTIME, OR ANYTIME, YOUR YOUNG CHILD WILL NEVER TIRE OF THIS SWEET STORY, AND NEITHER WILL YOU!

GOD'S HANDS & FEET
by Lisa Soland

In *God's Hands & Feet*, Fred's mother teaches him invaluable lessons on how to be "one of God's very important ambassadors." She explains, "You are to be God's hands and feet because when God wants to do something good in this world, He sometimes uses us to do it."

"Start children off on the way they should go, and even when they are old they will not turn from it." (Proverbs 22:6 NIV)

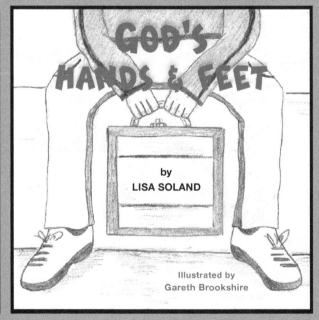

GOD'S HANDS & FEET

by
LISA SOLAND

Illustrated by
Gareth Brookshire

CPSIA information can be obtained
at www.ICGtesting.com
Printed in the USA
JSHW010346210521
15004JS00001B/6